101 conversation starters for couples

101 conversation starters for couples

GARY CHAPMAN

& RAMON PRESSON

Northfield Publishing
CHICAGO

We hope you enjoy this book from Northfield Publishing.
Our goal is to provide high quality, thought-provoking books
and products that connect truth to your real needs and challenges.
For more information on other books and products written
and produced from a biblical perspective, go to
www.moodypublishers.com or write to:

Northfield Publishing
820 N. LaSalle Boulevard
Chicago, IL 60610

5 7 9 10 8 6

Printed in the United States of America

Tips for Using 101 Conversation Starters

Your spouse is a fascinating person, a treasure trove of meaningful, humorous, and profound experiences, thoughts, feelings, ideas, memories, hopes, dreams, beliefs, and convictions. These questions celebrate the depth and wonderful mystery of your mate. Questions invite disclosure, and disclosure launches discovery. Discovery enriches a marriage and builds intimacy. Use the following 101 questions to prompt meaningful, in-depth discussions and to affirm and encourage your spouse.

Here are some ways to use the questions:

• During dinner at home (if you don't have children)

• During a quiet moment in the evening

• At bedtime (if both of you are alert)

• During dinner on a date night

• While in the car during a long drive

While the easiest way to proceed through the questions is to use them in the order they are presented, another possibility is that your spouse and you take turns in selecting the questions. We recommend that you do only one or two questions at a time. These questions are like dessert—a small and satisfying portion creates the anticipation for more later. *101 Conversation Starters for Couples* offers a process to enjoy, not a project to complete.

Have fun with these questions two or three times each week and watch intimacy grow in your marriage.

What are two things that happened today, and how did you feel about them?

What were some of your favorite toys as a child? What was your favorite candy?

Describe the home of one or both sets of your grandparents.

conversation starters for couples

What was something
you really wanted but were
not allowed to own as a
child or teen?

Describe one of your favorite elementary school teachers. Then describe a favorite high school teacher or college professor.

As you were growing up, what was unique about your family as compared to other families in your neighborhood or the families of your friends?

What was your most
serious physical injury
as a child or teen?

What do you remember
about learning to drive?

Can you recall visiting your parents' workplace?

If so, describe it and how you felt when you went there.

conversation starters for couples

Complete this sentence:

"I'm sure my mom and dad

wish I would . . . ."

What is perhaps the worst movie

you have ever seen?

conversation starters for couples

What tragic news story in the last few years made you particularly sad?

What was one of the most memorable weddings (other than your own) that you have attended?

What is something
you collected as
a child or teen?

What is a question that you wish you had the courage to ask your mother and/or father?

question

15

If you were given five acres
of land, where would you want it
to be and what would you
want to do with it?

question

16

conversation starters for couples

If you could own and operate your own business (and be guaranteed of its success), what would it be?

If you do not play a musical instrument, what one do you wish you could play? If you do/did play a musical instrument, do you recall how you chose that particular one?

What would you say are two of the best concerts you have seen, either in person or on video or film?

What are two of your all-time favorite movies (or books)?

My mother/father clearly did not understand what was considered cool when she/he bought me . . .

What famous person (deceased) would you like to have met?

Which of the following would
you find most gratifying?

☐ earning a PhD

☐ publishing a bestselling book

☐ recording an original chart-topping song

☐ winning an Olympic gold medal

If money and/or child care were no object, what would be your idea of the perfect New Year's Eve?

Who is one of the most genuinely spiritual persons you know?

How do you think the
world has changed since
September 11, 2001?

Which of the following rides

would be your first choice?

☐ a gondola in Venice

☐ a cab in London

☐ a Ferrari on the autobahn

☐ a hot air balloon in Switzerland

☐ an airboat in the Everglades

☐ a raft down the Colorado River

☐ a carriage in Paris

What is one of your favorite memories that includes snow?

Who was your favorite superhero or cartoon character?

If someone could bless you and pass on to you a special ability, who would you choose to bless you and with what ability?

Who is the most joyful

person you know?

Who is someone you wish you could infect with a more positive attitude?

Complete this sentence:

"It would make me a better person if

I were more like you in the way you . . ."

When in your life would you say
your self-esteem was the lowest?

Recall a time when you were given constructive criticism that proved beneficial.

The lion, beaver, otter, and golden retriever
are used to describe four personality types.
Which one do you think best describes you?

☐ Lion: strong, confident, leader, likes to make sure
things get done

☐ Beaver: detail oriented, organized, follows instructions,
good with projects

☐ Otter: very outgoing, enjoys people, humorous, creative

☐ Golden Retriever: loyal, sensitive, encouraging

If you could hire Martha Stewart

for a day, what would

you have her do?

Regardless of how long I live,

I hope I will always . . .

"It is more blessed to give than to receive."
Recall a gift that gave you considerable
satisfaction in presenting it.

Describe the location
and three features of
your dream home.

Who would you most like to

hear one of the following from?

"I love you."

"I support you."

"I respect you."

"I appreciate you."

"I miss you."

"I trust you."

In retrospect, what is something that your parents were wise in doing in raising you?

What was your most/least favorite subject in school?

If you could take a course in any subject

right now at your local college,

what type of course would it be?

In what way are you most/least

like your mother?

How are you most/least

like your father?

In Matthew 6:34, Jesus encourages us

to live with faith in the present.

Which is the greater obstacle for you?

☐ dwelling on the past

☐ worrying about the future

conversation starters for couples

Who was your best friend

in junior high school?

What did you do together?

As I was growing up,

my father was most like

☐ a coach　☐ a judge

☐ an historian　☐ a professor

☐ a preacher　☐ a manager

☐ a cheerleader

☐ other_____

If you inherited $200,000 (after taxes), what would you do with the money?

Name three jobs or careers

you are definitely not suited for.

Describe your pediatrician
when you were growing up.
What do you remember
about those doctor visits?

Concerning what biblical topic
or Bible passage (or verse)
do you wish you had a better
understanding?

What do you think that you will want to do in your retirement years?

Acts 2:42-47 describes a close, caring community. In what setting have you had the greatest experience of genuine fellowship?

☐ friends at school ☐ job where I worked ☐ sports team

☐ support group ☐ church-related group

☐ volunteer organization

☐ ministry/mission team ☐ fraternity/sorority

☐ other_____

question

54

conversation starters for couples

What item of clothing in my wardrobe do you really like to see me wear?

What is a song or
piece of music that moves
or inspires you?

What quality or skill that you possess would you find most gratifying to have your child imitate as an adult?

If you could win any
competition in the world,
what would it be?

What nonbiblical historical event would you like to have witnessed?

Name the Old Testament event
that you wish you could have witnessed.
Name the New Testament event (in addition
to the resurrection) that you wish
you could have witnessed.

question

60

conversation starters for couples

In TV's *The Andy Griffith Show*, Barney Fife once told Andy that the biggest purchase he ever made was a septic tank for his parents' wedding anniversary. What gift would you like to give to your parents?

What is something you thoroughly enjoyed doing as a child and have not done in years?

Richard Foster says that our lives are bombarded by hurry, crowds, and noise. Which of those three has been most bothersome for you lately?

Complete this sentence:
"A time that I felt I might
be in physical danger
was when . . ."

In what event would you most like to win an Olympic gold medal?

Recall a time when
you were disappointed
in not being chosen.

I wish I could hire _____

to write and record a song

from me to you.

I think I would crack under the torture

if I were forced to listen to only

_____ music all day and

could only eat _____ meals all day.

If we were to adopt a child

from another country,

which country would it be?

As a couple we make a great team, but it is most unlikely that we would ever team up to . . .

☐ win a mixed-doubles tennis championship

☐ sing a duet

☐ win a medal in couples figure skating

☐ be co-leaders (main speakers) of a nationally televised marriage seminar

☐ compete in a ballroom dancing competition

☐ operate a bed & breakfast

☐ co-author a book entitled *Stress-Free Parenting*

Imagine that your internal dashboard

has a spiritual passion gauge on it.

What is your present reading?

E _____

¼ _____

½ _____

¾ _____

F _____

What is the worst or most unusual job interview you ever had?

The circus act that most

reminds me of my job is . . .

What is your most/least favorite trait in others?

What kind of race best describes
your last seven days?

☐ BOSTON MARATHON *It seemed to last forever.*

☐ TOUR DE FRANCE *I was pedaling uphill as fast as I could.*

☐ KENTUCKY DERBY *I worked for so long on something that was over so quickly.*

☐ INDIANAPOLIS 500 *I went round and round, and I'm right where I started.*

☐ IRONMAN TRIATHLON *I endured a week full of job, family, and church activities.*

☐ 24 HOURS OF LE MANS *Sleep? What's that?*

☐ HUNDRED-METER HIGH HURDLES *All I did was sprint and navigate obstacles.*

☐ DEMOLITION DERBY *I feel beat up.*

Talk about your early experiences with someone of another race or nationality.

Describe a summer
camp experience.

What is your favorite
animated film?

When you were growing up,

where did your family go on vacations?

Describe one of those vacations.

Can you remember a time when you got lost or separated from your family or companions? Describe what happened and how you felt.

Recall a time when you got sick at a very inopportune time.

What high school or college course would you rather flee the country than be forced to take again?

Can you recall a first date during which you immediately knew there would not be a second date?

Select and describe a couple

who were friends with your parents

when you were growing up.

Recall a childhood memory
about one of the following:

- playing in a creek

- playing in a tree house

- catching fireflies

- running a lemonade stand

- pretending to be a superhero

- a slumber party or sleepover

- jumping off the high dive

Describe your parents' reaction
on the day you moved out
or left for college.

Recall something special about your high school or college graduation.

What is your favorite scene

from your favorite movie?

I thought it was one of the coolest items in my wardrobe at the time, but today I'm not sure I'd even wear it to a costume party. What is it?

Something I wanted to quit but my parents wouldn't let me was . . .

Joseph's brothers sold him into slavery. If you have siblings, what was one of the meanest things done to you by a brother or sister? If you are an only child, what was one of the meanest things done to you by a friend?

Describe someone you encountered recently who probably needs God in his or her life.

If you were offered the opportunity to be one of the contestants on *Survivor*, would you do it? If yes, what do you imagine would be the hardest thing for you to cope with?

One of the descendants of King Saul was named Mephibosheth. Do you like your first name? If you could choose another first name for yourself, what would it be?

In the movie *The Karate Kid*, young Daniel is befriended by an old Japanese man who teaches him karate, but more importantly offers him kindness and encouragement. Name an older person who blessed you with kindness and encouragement.

What is one of your
favorite stories that your
parents tell about you?

In the movie *Groundhog Day*, Bill Murray kept waking up only to repeat the same day over and over again. What recent day would you not want to repeat?

What old photograph of yourself makes you really laugh or cringe in embarrassment?

conversation starters for couples

Recall something about exchanging valentines when you were in elementary school.

Congratulations! Your boss just gave everyone a spring break. Where do you want to go?

100 conversation starters for couples

What is something that occurred this past year that you are especially thankful for?

 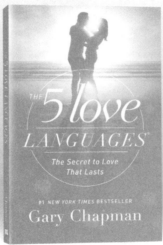 

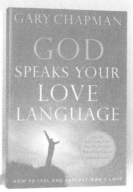

Learning your love language—and that of your spouse, teen, and child—might be the easiest and most important thing you ever learn. The assessments featured at www.5lovelanguages.com make it easy to discover your love language. Simply take one of our short profiles and find out how you and your loved one express and interpret love.

Right away, you can make a concerted effort to speak his or her primary language. It might not come naturally, but even the effort will be appreciated.

This dynamic site is also full of other helpful features—links to other resources, free stuff, upcoming events, podcasts, video, and more—all designed to encourage you and strengthen your relationships. We want to help you feel loved, and to effectively communicate love to others.

VISIT **5LOVELANGUAGES.COM**